MW00744119

TELEVISIONS

EVERYDAY INVENTIONS

Kristin Petrie
ABDO Publishing Company

visit us at
www.abdopublishing.com

Published by ABDO Publishing Company, 8000 West 78th Street, Edina, Minnesota 55439.
Copyright © 2009 by Abdo Consulting Group, Inc. International copyrights reserved in all
countries. No part of this book may be reproduced in any form without written permission from the
publisher. The Checkerboard Library™ is a trademark and logo of ABDO Publishing Company.

Printed in the United States.

Cover Photo: Getty Images
Interior Photos: Alamy pp. 15, 18, 26, 31; AP Images pp. 23, 27; Corbis pp. 8, 9, 10, 11, 29;
    iStockphoto pp. 1, 24; Getty Images pp. 5, 20; Megan M. Gunderson p. 14;
    Photo Researchers p. 13

Images on pages 17 and 19 reprinted with permission from *Britannica Student's Encyclopedia*,
    © 2007 by Encyclopædia Britannica, Inc.

Series Coordinator: Megan M. Gunderson
Editors: Megan M. Gunderson, BreAnn Rumsch
Art Direction & Cover Design: Neil Klinepier

Library of Congress Cataloging-in-Publication Data

Petrie, Kristin, 1970-
  Televisions / Kristin Petrie.
     p. cm. -- (Everyday inventions)
  Includes bibliographical references and index.
  ISBN 978-1-60453-089-6
  1. Television--Juvenile literature. 2. Television--Receivers and reception [--Juvenile literature. I.
Title.

  TK6640.P48 2009
  621.388--dc22

                                2008001562

CONTENTS

Televisions

Have you watched television today? Chances are, your answer is yes! Maybe you watched cartoons this morning or educational programs at school. Tonight, you might watch a movie or your favorite sports team.

The word *television* comes from Greek and Latin words meaning "far" and "to see." Seeing faraway things is exactly what television lets us do!

We often depend on television for news. It tells us what is happening in our community and beyond. Television also lets us see across oceans and even into space.

This amazing invention plays a huge role in our lives. It keeps us informed and entertained. Can you believe the television was invented less than 100 years ago? Keep reading to learn how it all began!

Television can be both entertaining and educational. Just make sure an adult always knows when, what, and how much you are watching.

Timeline

1921	Philo Taylor Farnsworth imagined an electronic television system.
1923	Vladimir Zworykin patented his idea for the iconoscope, a television transmission tube.
1924	Zworykin patented his idea for the kinescope, a cathode-ray television tube.
1925	John Logie Baird exhibited a mechanical television system.
1927	Farnsworth sent his first successful television image, a dollar sign.
1929	Using Zworykin's inventions, an all-electronic television system was exhibited.
1937	Engineer Allen Balcom Du Mont manufactured the first publicly available televisions.
1953	Color television was introduced.
1964	Color television sets became popular in the United States.
2009	The Federal Communications Commission stopped analog broadcasting in favor of digital broadcasting.

Television Facts

○ Have you ever heard television referred to as "the tube"? This nickname comes from a television's cathode-ray tube, which projects the picture onto the screen.

○ Closed captioning allows hearing impaired people to read on-screen what is being said on a television. It is also helpful in noisy places where someone can see but not hear a television. Closed captioning is sent as part of the television signal. The viewer turns it on, which is why it is called "closed" captioning. "Opening" the captioning is usually done with a remote control. This tells the television to decode the signal and display the words on-screen.

○ Do you ever wonder why your favorite show is no longer on the air? Surveying about 25,000 U.S. households, Nielsen Media Research tracks how many people watch a television program. This viewing information helps networks decide whether to keep or cancel a show.

Early Success

The first televisions were very different from today's televisions. In 1925, Scotsman John Logie Baird exhibited a mechanical television system.

In 1925, John Logie Baird used a mechanical television to send a live picture of a human face.

This system had moving parts. These included small motors and turning disks. Unfortunately, the system's tiny pictures were dim and blurry.

Meanwhile, 14-year-old Philo Taylor Farnsworth had imagined an electronic television system in 1921. His idea came from an advanced understanding of electricity.

Farnsworth believed images could be scanned and reproduced using **electrons**. This would replace spinning disks. The images could be of a much better quality. His system would be like a radio that transmitted pictures.

Philo Taylor Farnsworth held more than 160 patents for his various inventions.

Farnsworth's dream soon became reality. In 1927, he sent and received his first electronic television image. It was a dollar sign. Farnsworth's great success was celebrated.

Inventor Vladimir Zworykin had also been working on these new ideas. Zworykin had **patented** his idea for the iconoscope in 1923. This was a television transmission tube. In 1924, he patented the kinescope. This was a cathode-ray television tube.

Vladimir Zworykin is often considered the "Father of Modern Television."

With these two inventions, Zworykin created the first all-electronic television system. However, his system was not exhibited until 1929.

Electronic televisions used an amazing device called a cathode-ray tube (CRT). The CRT replaced the mechanical turning disk. It also improved image quality. Unfortunately, these televisions were too expensive for most people to afford.

Meanwhile, another inventor was working hard to advance the television. American Allen Balcom Du Mont is known for improving the CRT. In 1937, Du Mont also manufactured the first publicly available televisions.

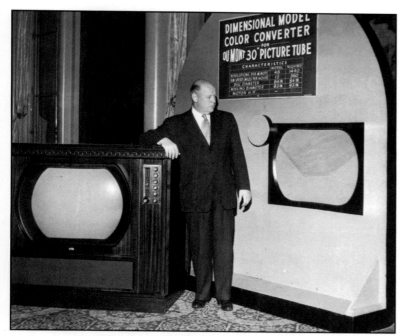

Allen Balcom Du Mont's advancements helped lower the cost of televisions.

During the 1950s, the popularity of televisions exploded! In 1950, just 9 percent of U.S. households had a television. But by 1955, 78 percent of households had one.

In 1953, color television was introduced. Color television sets became popular in the United States around 1964.

The first remote controls were introduced around the same time. Thanks to many great modern minds, televisions continue to advance rapidly today.

Bits and Pieces

There is more to a television than a screen and a remote control. Lots of parts work together so you can watch your favorite programs.

Let's start at your television's antenna. This is where the television **signal** enters your television. It is made up of both picture and sound signals. After entering the television, their first stop is an **amplifier**. This device strengthens the signals.

The decoder then turns the picture, or video, signal into three separate signals. The signals continue their journey with the help of **electron** guns. These are not really guns. They simply get their name from their job. Electron guns shoot electron beams at the television screen. They help re-create the original images.

The electron guns are located at one end of your television's picture tube. Your television's glass screen is at the other end. Chemicals called phosphors coat the inside of the screen. The

electron beams hit the phosphors. This action forms the pictures on your screen.

Last but not least is the speaker. This part uses the sound, or audio, **signal** to re-create the original sounds. That way, you can hear what your favorite actors are saying. All these parts work together to make television a fun invention!

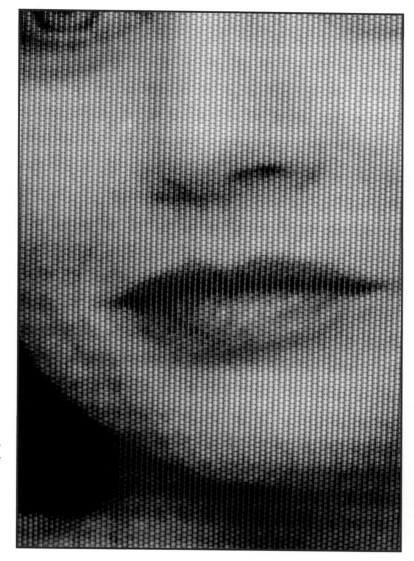

Phosphors glow red, green, or blue. Together, they reproduce all the colors and patterns in a televised image.

Parts of a Television

ANTENNA

SCREEN

POWER CORD

VIDEO CASSETTE
RECORDER (VCR)

REMOTE CONTROL

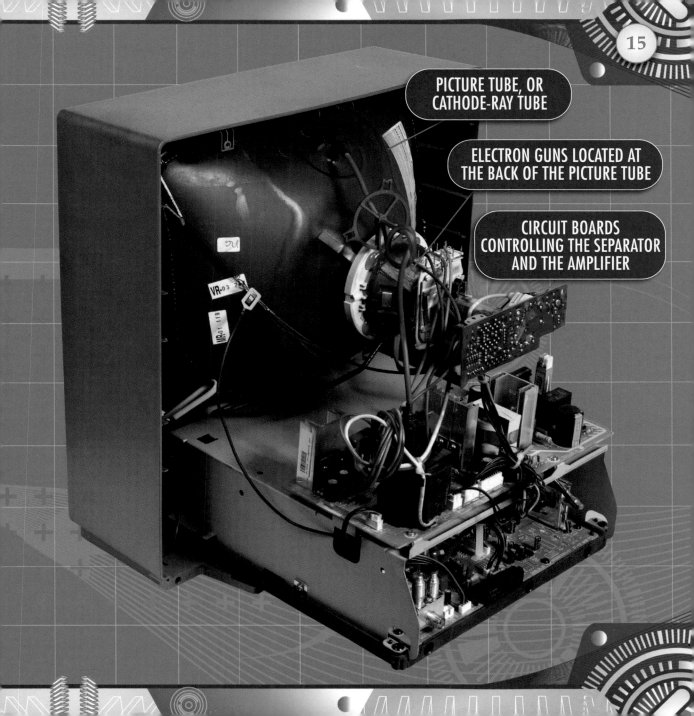

PICTURE TUBE, OR CATHODE-RAY TUBE

ELECTRON GUNS LOCATED AT THE BACK OF THE PICTURE TUBE

CIRCUIT BOARDS CONTROLLING THE SEPARATOR AND THE AMPLIFIER

Television Signals

You're probably starting to see how television parts work together. Let's look closer. How do your favorite shows appear on your television set at home?

It all begins with capturing images and sounds. This is done with a television camera and a sound recording system. Light bounces off images. Then, it enters the camera through a lens. Inside the camera, filters and mirrors divide the light into three primary colors. These are red, green, and blue.

Next, an image sensor scans each color **signal** into lines. It also creates three separate electronic signals. This is done in camera tubes or by **charge-coupled devices**. Then, the signals are **amplified**.

These amplified, scanned images enter an encoder next. The encoder combines the three signals. It also adds other signals. These help your television understand what it receives.

Once combined, the electronic picture **signals** move to a transmitter. The transmitter combines the picture and sound signals. This creates a television signal. Then, the transmitter sends the combined signal to an antenna. From there, the television signal is broadcast out into the air!

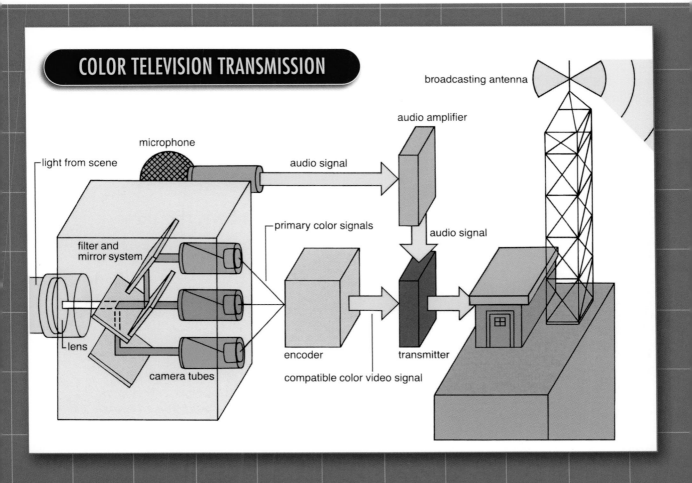

COLOR TELEVISION TRANSMISSION

broadcasting antenna

audio amplifier

microphone

audio signal

light from scene

primary color signals

audio signal

filter and mirror system

lens

encoder

transmitter

camera tubes

compatible color video signal

Television **signals** travel through the air as **electromagnetic waves**. The signals hit a receiving antenna. It brings them down into your television. Then, a tuner sorts through all the signals hitting your antenna. It selects only the signal for the channel you've chosen to watch.

Several things must still happen before an image appears on the screen. Inside your television, the chosen signal passes through a group of electronic circuits. First, an **amplifier** strengthens the television signal. Then, a separator splits the television signal back into image and sound signals.

The image signal moves to a decoder. This device splits it back into three signals. Then, the decoder sends the three image signals to the picture tube.

From here, the three **electron** guns shoot them toward the screen. The electron beams pass through

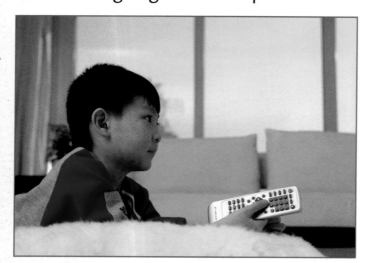

A remote control can tell your television's tuner exactly which channel you would like to watch.

the shadow mask first. This metal plate has holes. They direct each beam to hit only its matching color phosphor.

At the same time, the sound **signal** is **amplified**. Then, the television speaker turns it into sound waves. Together with the images, this re-creates the original program on your television screen.

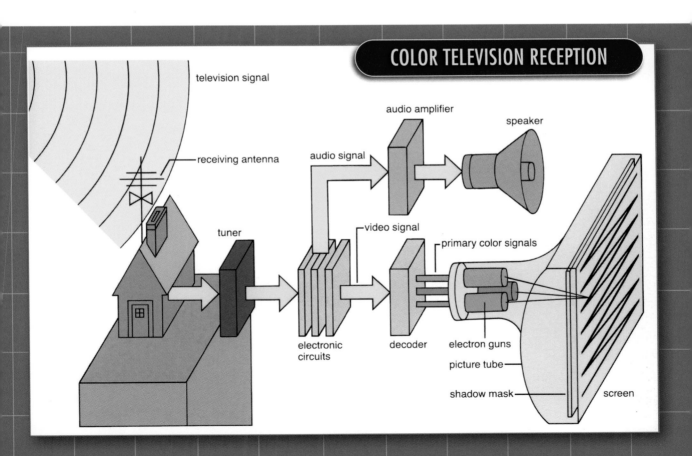

COLOR TELEVISION RECEPTION

television signal

receiving antenna

tuner

audio signal

audio amplifier

speaker

video signal

primary color signals

electronic circuits

decoder

electron guns

picture tube

shadow mask

screen

Digital Future

Today more than ever, there are numerous televisions to choose from. Buying the right television takes research! Most televisions are grouped by how they get their **signals**. Let's look at the different ways early and modern televisions do this.

Some new televisions are so light and flat they can be hung on a wall!

Most older televisions depend on analog **signals**. This type of broadcasting transmits information by sending television signals as waves.

However, **digital** television has been replacing the analog system. It transmits image and sound signals as ones and zeros. This allows more information to be transmitted to your television at once.

Digital television provides greater broadcasting possibilities. For example, a broadcaster can send multiple programs on one channel. These signals are also stronger and more dependable than analog signals.

High-definition television is a digitally broadcast signal. It provides sharper picture and sound quality. And, most high-definition televisions have wider screens like at a movie theater.

In February 2009, the **Federal Communications Commission** stopped analog broadcasting. Instead, only digital broadcasting became available in the United States. Today, new televisions contain digital tuners. That way, they can receive the new broadcasts.

Tubes to Plasma

The televisions your grandparents watched had CRTs. These devices still operate basic televisions today. CRT televisions are generally affordable. However, they can be big and heavy.

Liquid crystal display (LCD) televisions do not have a CRT. Instead, electric **signals** activate a liquid crystal in the television. This displays the images.

LCDs are more expensive than CRT televisions. They also remain difficult to produce in large sizes. However, their lightweight, flat design makes them popular.

Plasma televisions also feature a flat screen, or panel. These televisions have two glass plates with gas between them. The gas is usually a mixture of xenon and either neon or helium.

An electric **current** is added to the gas. The gas forms a kind of plasma, which puts out **ultraviolet** light. This causes

Today, even automobiles may have televisions with LCD screens!

the phosphors on the screen to create visible light. That means you can see what is being broadcast. The process makes bright, clear pictures for the viewer.

Broadcasting

The simplest way to send and receive a television **signal** is with antennas. A broadcasting antenna sends out the television signal. The signal rides along a carrier wave to a receiving antenna. This antenna brings the signal to the attached television. There, the signal is separated back into images and sounds.

Cable television was developed in the 1950s. It solves the problem of mountains, tall buildings, and other television signal blockers. A high-powered community antenna or a **satellite** dish receives the broadcast signals. The signals are then directed to cables. These stretch out through the community to individual homes.

Satellite dishes must be aimed at the correct satellite to receive television signals.

Other homes receive television **signals** directly from **satellites**. Direct broadcast satellite (DBS) television also transmits signals using radio waves.

Instead of putting signals into cables, the satellite television company sends them to satellites in space. From there, the signals go directly to homes with receiving satellite dishes. A satellite dish acts like a specially designed antenna. Usually, customers have to pay a fee for cable and satellite services.

TYPES OF TELEVISION BROADCASTING

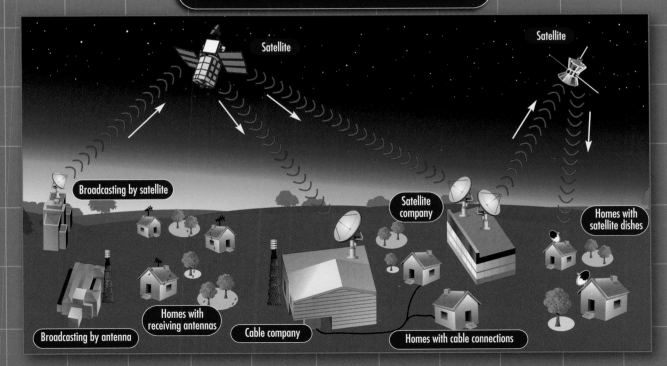

Satellite

Satellite

Broadcasting by satellite

Satellite company

Homes with satellite dishes

Homes with receiving antennas

Cable company

Broadcasting by antenna

Homes with cable connections

Behind the Scenes

Most of us watch television for entertainment. Some admire the actors or the special effects they see on-screen. Still others are interested in how their televisions work.

Do actual television shows catch your interest? You could become a television producer, a director, or even an actor. Producers oversee everything it takes to make a television program. They approve content, money, directors, and actors.

Once hired, the director controls the show. This includes giving direction to camera operators, stage managers, and actors. Acting is a competitive profession!

Many schools offer classes in television production. Students can learn to direct, operate cameras, act, and more.

Television salespeople stay informed about this constantly improving technology.

Therefore, hard work and talent are important to an actor's success.

Not all jobs are in television broadcasting. Scientists help design new televisions. They also help improve how this ever-changing invention works. Repair experts also learn how televisions work. With this knowledge, you could repair your own television if it broke!

Endless Choices

Now you know how televisions work. But do you think television is good or bad? People have many different opinions about this.

On the one hand, television brings us news and weather. It shows us live pictures of places we may never visit. Television also provides heartwarming, educational, and interesting programs. These help us understand people from other parts of the world.

On the other hand, we risk spending too much time watching television. It is entertaining! There are hundreds of television channels. And the average American child spends four hours each day in front of the television. This time could be spent exercising outdoors, reading, or talking with family.

In addition, some scientists argue that violence on television could be unhealthy. They say it may make a person more likely to accept violence in society. Therefore, a

One benefit of television technology is videoconferencing. For example, the U.S. president can meet with soldiers overseas without ever leaving Washington, D.C.

responsible adult should always know what you are watching. With careful use, television will remain one of the most important inventions of all time!

GLOSSARY

amplify - to increase the strength of. An amplifier is a device for increasing the strength of electronic signals.

charge-coupled device - an image sensor that builds up electric charges as light from an image hits it. The charges are then released as an electric current. This can be translated by computers and other devices to re-create the image.

current - the flow of electricity.

digital - of or relating to numerical data that can be read by a computer.

electromagnetic wave - a wave made up of electric and magnetic effects, such as a radio wave or an X-ray.

electron - one of the main parts of an atom. It is negatively charged and travels around the nucleus, or center, of an atom.

Federal Communications Commission - a U.S. government organization in charge of regulating communications, such as those by radio, television, or satellite.

patent - the exclusive right granted to a person to make or sell an invention for a certain period of time.

satellite - a manufactured object that orbits Earth.

signal - a sound or an image transmitted in electronic communication, such as radio, telephone, or television. A signal is the wave or the current that transmits the message as well. Also, a signal may simply be an indication of something.

ultraviolet - a type of light that cannot be seen with the human eye.

WEB SITES

To learn more about televisions, visit ABDO Publishing Company on the World Wide Web at **www.abdopublishing.com**. Web sites about televisions are featured on our Book Links page. These links are routinely monitored and updated to provide the most current information available.

INDEX